Descendants of Thomas Weatherly

Generation 1

1. **THOMAS[1] WEATHERLY** . He died on 28 Mar 1739 in St. John's Parish, Colleton County, South Carolina. He married **SARAH WAIGHT**.

More About Thomas Weatherly:
Occupation: Planter

Notes for Thomas Weatherly:
Will Probated April 28, 1749.

Thomas Weatherly and Sarah Waight had the following children:

2.   i. WILLIAM[2] WEATHERLY. He died on 19 May 1761 in Charleston, South Carolina. He married SARAH COLE.

        ii.   SARAH WEATHERLY.

        iii. MARY ANN WEATHERLY. She married BENJAMIN COWAN.

3.   iv. CATHERINE WEATHERLY. She died on 29 Oct 1750. She married WILLIAM FERGUSON.

4.   v.   THOMAS WEATHERLY. He died in 1749 in Colleton, South Carolina. He married MARY (UNKNOWN).

5.   vi. ISAAC WEATHERLY was born on 13 Oct 1718. He died on 18 Jan 1765 in St. Helena's Parish, Granville County, South Carolina. He married Martha Fripp, daughter of John Fripp and Martha Jenkins on 07 Dec 1754 in St. Helena's Parish, Granville County,South Carolina. She was born on 31 May 1728. She died on 16 Nov 1783.

        vii. GEORGE WEATHERLY. He married Mary Conyears on 01 Jan 1763 in St. Helena's Parish, Granville County,South Carolina.

        viii. ROBERT WEATHERLY was born on 18 Mar 1739.

        ix.   ELIZABETH WEATHERLY was born on 26 Aug 1736.

Generation 2

2. **WILLIAM[2] WEATHERLY** (Thomas[1]). He died on 19 May 1761 in Charleston, South Carolina. He married **SARAH COLE**.

William Weatherly and Sarah Cole had the following children:

6.   i. ISAAC[3] WEATHERLY was born about 1756 in South Carolina. He married STATIRA COOK. She was born on 21 Sep 1761 in Wallingford, Connecticut. She died on 10 Jan 1802 in Charleston, South Carolina.

        ii.   SARAH WEATHERLY. She married WILLIAM ADAMS.

        iii. WILLIAM WEATHERLY.

        iv.   MARY WEATHERLY was born about 1740 in John's Island, South Carolina.

3. CATHERINE[2] WEATHERLY (Thomas[1]). She died on 29 Oct 1750. She married WILLIAM FERGUSON.

    William Ferguson and Catherine Weatherly had the following children:
    i.   MARY[3] FERGUSON.

    ii. SARAH FERGUSON.

    iii. WILLIAM FERGUSON.

4. THOMAS[2] WEATHERLY (Thomas[1]). He died in 1749 in Colleton, South Carolina. He married MARY (UNKNOWN).

    Notes for Thomas Weatherly:
    Will Dated March 28, 1749.
    Will Proven April 28, 1749.

    Thomas Weatherly and Mary (unknown) had the following child:
    i.   MARY[3] WEATHERLY.

5. ISAAC[2] WEATHERLY (Thomas[1]) was born on 13 Oct 1718. He died on 18 Jan 1765 in St. Helena's Parish, Granville County, South Carolina. He married Martha Fripp, daughter of John Fripp and Martha Jenkins on 07 Dec 1754 in St. Helena's Parish, Granville County, South Carolina. She was born on 31 May 1728. She died on 16 Nov 1783.

    More About Isaac Weatherly:
    Occupation: Planter

    Notes for Isaac Weatherly: Will
    Signed January 18, 1765. Will
    Proven October 23, 1765.

    South Carolina Marriages 1688-1799
    Weatherly, Isaac & Martha Waight, widow, 7 Dec.
    1754. St. Hel. Pr.

    More About Isaac Weatherly and Martha Fripp:
    Marriage Fact: Martha Fripp was the widow of Isaac Waight when she married Isaac Weatherly.

    Isaac Weatherly and Martha Fripp had the following child:
    i.   ISAAC[3] WEATHERLY. He died in 1768.

Generation 3

6. ISAAC[3] WEATHERLY (William[2], Thomas[1]) was born about 1756 in South Carolina. He married STATIRA COOK. She was born on 21 Sep 1761 in Wallingford, Connecticut. She died on 10 Jan 1802 in Charleston, South Carolina.

    More About Isaac Weatherly:
    Military Service: Revolutionary War - South Carolina

Notes for Isaac Weatherly:
Served as Lieutenant and then Captain in 1st South Carolina Regiment. Joined in May 1776 and was captured at Charleston, South Carolina on May 12, 1780.

More About Statira Cook:
Cause Of Death: Yellow Fever

Notes for Statira Cook:
Buried on January 10, 1801, probably died from yellow fever.

Isaac Weatherly and Statira Cook had the following children:

7. i. WILLIAM W.⁴ WEATHERLY was born on 16 May 1786 in South Carolina. He died on 26 Feb 1866 in Lone Oak, Hunt County, Texas. He married (1) FRANCES SMITH on 28 Nov 1818 in Greene County, Georgia. She was born on 18 Jan 1798 in North Carolina. She died on 05 Dec 1877 in Lone Oak, Hunt County, Texas. He married (2) ELIZABETH SMITH, daughter of Joseph Smith and Sarah (unknown) on 16 May 1811 in Clarke County, Georgia. She was born in Georgia. She died before 1818 in Georgia.

ii. ISAAC WEATHERLY was born in 1782 in South Carolina. He died on 20 Jun 1805 in Charleston, South Carolina. He married Rachel Rambert on 14 Aug 1804 in Charleston, South Carolina.

More About Isaac Weatherly:
Occupation: Bricklayer

Notes for Isaac Weatherly:
Married on August 14, 1804. August 18, 1804 is date of newspaper reporting the wedding.

iii. JOHN WEATHERLY. He died on 07 Oct 1801 in Charleston, South Carolina.

More About John Weatherly:
Cause Of Death: Yellow Fever

iv. SARAH C. WEATHERLY was born about 1784 in Charleston, South Carolina. She married Phillip Frazer on 15 Apr 1804 in Charleston, South Carolina.

Generation 4

7. **WILLIAM W.⁴ WEATHERLY** (Isaac³, William², Thomas¹) was born on 16 May 1786 in South Carolina. He died on 26 Feb 1866 in Lone Oak, Hunt County, Texas. He married (1) **FRANCES SMITH** on 28 Nov 1818 in Greene County, Georgia. She was born on 18 Jan 1798 in North Carolina. She died on 05 Dec 1877 in Lone Oak, Hunt County, Texas. He married (2) **ELIZABETH SMITH**, daughter of Joseph Smith and Sarah (unknown) on 16 May 1811 in Clarke County, Georgia. She was born in Georgia. She died before 1818 in Georgia.

More About William W. Weatherly:
Burial: Hall Cemetery, Lone Oak, Hunt County, Texas
Occupation: 1850 in Militia District 858, Paulding County, Georgia; Brick Layer

More About Frances Smith:
Burial: Hall Cemetery, Lone Oak, Hunt County, Texas
Living In: 1870 With her son, Thomas, and his wife in Precinct 4, Hunt County, Texas.

William W. Weatherly and Frances Smith had the following children:

    i.   MATILDA T.[5] WEATHERLY was born in 1820 in Clarke County, Georgia. She married Miles Yandle on 15 Jul 1858 in Rusk County, Texas. He was born in 1815 in North Carolina. He died on 31 Aug 1863 in Rusk County, Texas.

        More About Matilda T. Weatherly:
        Living In: 1850 With her parents in Militia District 858, Paulding County, Georgia.
        Living In: 1870 With her brother, Thomas, and his wife in Precinct 4, Hunt County, Texas.

8.   ii. AUGUSTUS GRAHAM WEATHERLY was born on 25 Feb 1826 in Clarke County, Georgia. He died on 08 Jan 1886 in Lone Oak, Hunt County, Texas. He married Elizabeth Jane Harrison, daughter of John Harrison and Rhoda Gordon on 28 Sep 1847 in Paulding County, Georgia. She was born on 27 May 1830 in South Carolina. She died on 09 Oct 1908 in Hunt County, Texas.

9.   iii. DAVID S. WEATHERLY was born about 1827 in Clarke County, Georgia. He married Ann America Beall, daughter of Francis Marion Beall and Sidney Elizabeth Sheppard on 01 Oct 1857 in Rusk County, Texas. She was born about 1842 in Georgia.

10.   iv. SARAH C. WEATHERLY was born on 21 Jul 1830 in Clarke County, Georgia. She died on 10 Jul 1907 in Lone Oak, Texas. She married Thornton Pollard, son of John Pollard and Elizabeth Strong on 20 Jan 1853 in Polk County, Georgia. He was born on 14 Apr 1831 in Georgia. He died on 10 Jul 1910 in McKinney, Collin County, Texas.

    v. THOMAS S. WEATHERLY was born on 13 Nov 1831 in Clarke County, Georgia. He died on 01 Mar 1913 in Lone Oak, Hunt County, Texas. He married Frances Jane Rawley, daughter of Darius Rawley and Purlina McCraw on 18 Oct 1866 in Hunt County, Texas. She was born on 19 Feb 1843 in North Carolina. She died on 16 Sep 1916 in Navasota, Grimes County, Texas.

        More About Thomas S. Weatherly:
        Burial: Lone Oak Cemetery, Lone Oak, Hunt County, Texas
        Occupation: 1860 in Precinct 1, Dallas County, Texas; Carpenter
        Occupation: 1870 in Precinct 4, Hunt County, Texas; Farmer
        Occupation: 1880 in Precinct 4, Hunt County, Texas; Farmer
        Occupation: 1900 in Justice Precinct 1, Rains County, Texas; Farmer
        Military Service: 02 Oct 1861 in Camp Reeves, Grayson County, Texas; Enlisted in Company H, 11th Texas Cavalry, C.S.A. (Young's Regiment, 3rd Texas Cavalry)

11.   vi. FRANCES M. WEATHERLY was born on 07 Feb 1835 in Clarke County, Georgia. She died on 29 Apr 1918 in Hunt County, Texas. She married John A. Schenck on 30 Mar 1856 in Rusk County, Texas. He was born on 25 Dec 1828 in Virginia. He died on 28 Jul 1871 in Hunt County, Texas.

William W. Weatherly and Elizabeth Smith had the following children:

12.   vii. WILLIAM SANFORD WEATHERLY was born on 12 Mar 1812 in Clarke County, Georgia. He died on 08 Dec 1889 in Athens, Clarke County, Georgia. He married Elizabeth Nance on 30 Aug 1838 in Randolph County, Georgia. She was born on 01 Jan 1820 in Georgia. She died on 01 May 1890 in Athens, Georgia.

13.   viii. JOSEPH JUDGE WEATHERLY was born on 18 Feb 1813 in Clarke County, Georgia. He died on 24 Mar 1888 in Benton County, Tennessee. He married (1) VIRGINIA VINSON WOODSON on 31 Jan 1839 in Henry County, Tennessee. She was born on 04 Apr 1824 in Tennessee. She died on 30 Nov 1857. He married (2) MARGARET M. HUGHES on 10 Nov 1858 in Henry County, Tennessee. She was born about 1826 in North Carolina. She died on 27 Jan 1897 in Benton County, Tennessee.

14.   ix. STATIRAH ELIZABETH WEATHERLY was born on 05 Oct 1815 in Clarke County, Georgia. She died on 21 Sep 1897 in Catoosa County, Georgia. She married William Madison Nance, son of John Nance and Elizabeth Ryan on 19 Jun 1835 in Clarke County, Georgia. He was born on 18 Dec 1809 in Georgia. He died on 11 Apr 1863 in Catoosa County, Georgia.

15.   x. ISAAC C. WEATHERLY was born on 15 Jun 1817 in Clarke County, Georgia. He died on 15 Aug 1887 in Lone Oak, Hunt County, Texas. He married Rachael A. Crabb, daughter of James Burton Crabb and Rachel Jones on 14 Feb 1839 in Henry County, Georgia. She was born on 22 Dec 1822 in Columbia County, Georgia. She died on 08 Sep 1896 in Lone Oak, Hunt County, Texas.

Generation 5

8. **AUGUSTUS GRAHAM**[5] **WEATHERLY** (William W.[4], Isaac[3], William[2], Thomas[1]) was born on 25 Feb 1826 in Clarke County, Georgia. He died on 08 Jan 1886 in Lone Oak, Hunt County, Texas. He married Elizabeth Jane Harrison, daughter of John Harrison and Rhoda Gordon on 28 Sep 1847 in Paulding County, Georgia. She was born on 27 May 1830 in South Carolina. She died on 09 Oct 1908 in Hunt County, Texas.

More About Augustus Graham Weatherly:
Burial: 10 Jan 1886 in East Mount Cemetery, Greenville, Hunt County, Texas
Occupation: 1850 in Militia District 858, Paulding County, Georgia; Farmer
Occupation: 1860 in Beat 12, Rusk County, Texas; Farmer
Occupation: 1880 in Precinct 4, Hunt County, Texas; Farmer
Military Service: 12 Sep 1863 in Greenville, Hunt County, Texas; Enlisted for six months in Company E, 2nd Cavalry, Texas State Troops, C.S.A.
Property: 1880 in Hunt County, Texas; 26 Acres Improved

Notes for Augustus Graham Weatherly:
Will Dated September 7, 1883.
Will Filed February 1, 1886.
Will Recorded March 2, 1888

Came to Texas in 1857

January 10, 1886 in the Galveston Daily
News Death of an Esteemed Citizen
GREENVILLE, January 9 - Mr. A. G. Weatherly, county treasurer of Hunt County, died of pneumonia in this city last night, after an illness of only a week. He was a worthy and most

excellent gentlemean and citizen, as has been attested by his being elected twice to the office he held. His remains were taken to Lone Oak tonight for interment there to-morrow by the Masonic fraternity.

Dallas (Texas) Morning News, Sun, 10 Jan 1886, page
9: Death of A.G. Weatherly
Special to The News.
GREENVILLE, Jan. 9.- Mr. A. G. Weatherly, County Treasurer of Hunt County, died of pneumonia in this city last evening, after an illness of only a week. He was a most excellent gentleman and had been elected twice to the office he held. His remains were taken to Lone Oak to-night for interment by the Masonic fraternity.

More About Elizabeth Jane Harrison:
Burial: East Mount Cemetery, Greenville, Hunt County, Texas
Living In: 04 Jun 1900 Living in the household of Charles Edward Savage in Whitewright, Grayson County, Texas.
Living In: 07 Jun 1900 Living with her son. William, and his family in Whitewright, Grayson County, Texas.

Notes for Elizabeth Jane Harrison:
Came to Texas in 18557.

Augustus Graham Weatherly and Elizabeth Jane Harrison had the following children:

16.   i. MARY FRANCIS[6] WEATHERLY was born on 19 Sep 1848 in Paulding County, Georgia. She died on 10 Apr 1915 in Denton, Texas. She married William Payne, son of Nathan Payne and Mary Elizabeth Glass on 06 Dec 1865 in Hunt County, Texas. He was born on 06 Nov 1842 in Barren County, Kentucky. He died on 02 Nov 1909 in Denton, Texas.

17.   ii. SARAH ELIZABETH WEATHERLY was born on 06 Feb 1850 in Cedartown, Polk County, Georgia. She died on 02 Feb 1942 in Victoria, Victoria County, Texas. She married Robert Pinkney Rawley, son of Darius Rawley and Purlina McCraw on 14 Feb 1867 in Lone Oak, Hunt County, Texas. He was born on 30 May 1841 in Reedsville, North Carolina. He died on 18 Jan 1915 in Victoria, Texas.

18.   iii. JAMES A. WEATHERLY was born on 20 Sep 1855 in Paulding County, Georgia. He died on 07 Apr 1899 in Greeneville, Texas. He married Edna Paralee Horn on 04 Nov 1877 in Hunt County, Texas. She was born on 15 Apr 1858 in Texas. She died on 06 Apr 1910 in Greeneville, Texas.

19.   iv. A. MATILDA WEATHERLY was born in 1858 in Texas. She died after 15 Apr 1910. She married T. H. Green on 22 Nov 1876 in Hunt County, Texas. He was born about 1850 in South Carolina. He died before 15 Apr 1910.

20.   v. GEORGIA VIRGINIA WEATHERLY was born on 08 Jun 1863 in Lone Oak, Texas. She died on 25 Jul 1919 in Celeste, Hunt County, Texas. She married Auburn Monroe Neal, son of Joseph James Neal and Martha Glover Garrett on 13 Oct 1880 in Lone Oak, Texas. He was born on 15 Aug 1859 in Callaway County, Missouri. He died on 20 Nov 1933 in Zephyr, Brown County, Texas.

21.   vi. TOMMY DELLA WEATHERLY was born on 02 Dec 1868 in Texas. She died on 02 Dec 1961 in Houston, Harris County, Texas. She married (1) JAMES ANDERSON TAYLOR, son of S. W. Taylor and Martha A. (unknown) on 23 Sep 1933 in Hunt County, Texas. He was born on 04 Mar 1861 in Alabama. He died on 27 Jun 1956 in Celeste, Hunt County, Texas. She married (2) RICHARD WARREN on 18 Dec 1887 in Hunt County, Texas. He was born in 1856 in Mississippi. She married (3) WILLIAM J. MCNATT on 16 Dec 1897 in Hunt County, Texas. He was born on 04 Dec 1853 in Tennessee. He died on 10 Apr 1924.

       vii. JOHN G. WEATHERLY was born on 22 Feb 1871 in Texas. He died on 21 May 1959 in Ventura County, California. He married Bessie Lenore Bendel on 26 Nov 1899 in Hunt County, Texas. She was born on 07 Sep 1877 in Kentucky. She died on 06 Oct 1956 in Ventura County, California.

       More About John G. Weatherly:
       Occupation: 1900 in Greenville, Hunt County, Texas; Hardware Salesman
       Occupation: 1910 in Texico, Curry County, New Mexico; Farmer
       Occupation: 1930 in Santa Paula, Ventura County, California; Proprietor of Variety Store
       Occupation: 1940 in Santa Paula, Ventura County, California; Furniture Repair Work

9. DAVID S.[5] WEATHERLY (William W.[4], Isaac[3], William[2], Thomas[1]) was born about 1827 in Clarke County, Georgia. He married Ann America Beall, daughter of Francis Marion Beall and Sidney Elizabeth Sheppard on 01 Oct 1857 in Rusk County, Texas. She was born about 1842 in Georgia.

More About David S. Weatherly:
Living In: 1850 With his parents in Militia Districrt 858, Paulding County, Georgia.
Living In: 1860 Next door to his wife's parents.
Living In: 1862 Henderson, Rusk County, Texas
Occupation: 1850 in Militia District 858, Paulding County, Georgia; Laborer
Occupation: 1860 in Beat 12, Rusk County, Texas; Farmer
Military Service: 10 May 1862 in Camp Sidney Johnson, Marion County, Texas; Enlisted in Company I, 18th Texas Infantry, C.S.A.

David S. Weatherly and Ann America Beall had the following child:
       i.   S. E.[6] WEATHERLY was born in 1859 in Rusk County, Texas.

10. SARAH C.[5] WEATHERLY (William W.[4], Isaac[3], William[2], Thomas[1]) was born on 21 Jul 1830 in Clarke County, Georgia. She died on 10 Jul 1907 in Lone Oak, Texas. She married Thornton Pollard, son of John Pollard and Elizabeth Strong on 20 Jan 1853 in Polk County, Georgia. He was born on 14 Apr 1831 in Georgia. He died on 10 Jul 1910 in McKinney, Collin County, Texas.

More About Sarah C. Weatherly:
Burial: Lone Oak Cemetery, Lone Oak, Hunt County, Texas

More About Thornton Pollard:
Burial: Lone Oak Cemetery, Lone Oak, Hunt County, Texas
Living In: 1850 With his mother in Militia District 848, Paulding County, Georgia
Living In: 1910 With his daughter, Clara, and her husband in Lone Oak, Hunt County, Texas.
Occupation: 1850 in Militia District 848, Paulding County, Georgia; Farmer
Occupation: 1860 in Precinct 9, Hunt County, Texas; Farmer
Occupation: 1870 in Precinct 4, Hunt County, Texas; Farmer

Occupation: 1880 in Precinct 4, Hunt County, Texas; Farmer
Occupation: 1900 in Lone Oak, Hunt County, Texas; Retired
Occupation: 1910 in Lone Oak, Hunt County, Texas; Retired

Notes for Thornton Pollard:
Death certificate has July 10, 1910 for date of death. Headstone has July 5, 1910 for date of death.

Thornton Pollard and Sarah C. Weatherly had the following children:

  i. JOHN W.[6] POLLARD was born about 1853 in Georgia.

22. ii. ALICE POLLARD was born about 1855 in Texas. She died in Lone Oak, Texas. She married Thomas Joseph Bell on 29 Jun 1879 in Hunt County, Texas. He was born in 1854. He died in 1899 in Lone Oak, Texas.

  iii. CLARA FRANCES POLLARD was born on 15 Aug 1857 in Texas. She died on 21 Apr 1942 in Lone Oak, Hunt County, Texas. She married Isham Lynch on 21 Sep 1880 in Harrison County, Texas. He was born on 04 Feb 1842. He died on 16 Jul 1912 in Lone Oak, Texas.

  More About Clara Frances Pollard:
  Burial: 22 Apr 1942 in Lone Oak Cemetery, Lone Oak, Hunt County, Texas
  Living In: 22 Jun 1880 in With her parents in Precinct 4, Hunt County, Texas.

23. iv. JAMES RALSTON POLLARD was born in Nov 1858 in Texas. He died in 1943 in Lone Oak, Texas. He married Carrie Lee McFadden, daughter of Sam McFadden and Nettie Hardin on 14 Jan 1883 in Rains County, Texas. She was born in Jan 1862 in Texas. She died on 27 Aug 1939 in Lone Oak, Texas.

24. v. THOMAS A. POLLARD was born on 27 Jun 1861 in Lone Oak, Texas. He died on 23 Mar 1937. He married MOLLIE A. ALLEN. She was born in 1862 in Louisiana. She died on 23 Mar 1911.

  vi. CHARLES C. POLLARD was born in Sep 1866 in Lone Oak, Texas. He married STELLA MURPHY. She was born in Dec 1874 in Missouri. He married (2) MARY M. CARR on 12 Sep 1886 in Hunt County, Texas. She was born in Texas.

25. vii. REESE DAVID POLLARD was born in Sep 1869 in Lone Oak, Texas. He married Jessie Goff in 1893. She was born in Apr 1875 in Texas.

11. **FRANCES M.**[5] **WEATHERLY** (William W.[4], Isaac[3], William[2], Thomas[1]) was born on 07 Feb 1835 in Clarke County, Georgia. She died on 29 Apr 1918 in Hunt County, Texas. She married John A. Schenck on 30 Mar 1856 in Rusk County, Texas. He was born on 25 Dec 1828 in Virginia. He died on 28 Jul 1871 in Hunt County, Texas.

More About Frances M. Weatherly:
Burial: Lone Oak Cemetery, Lone Oak, Hunt County, Texas
Living In: 1900 With her son, William, and his family in Lone Oak, Hunt County, Texas.
Living In: 1910 With her son, William, and his family in Lone Oak, Hunt County, Texas.

Notes for Frances M. Weatherly:
Birth and death dates are from headstone.

More About John A. Schenck:
Burial: Hall Cemetery, Lone Oak, Hunt County, Texas
Occupation: 1850 in District 8, Botetourt County, Virginia; Wagon Maker
Occupation: 1860 in Precinct 3, Hunt County, Texas; Mechanic
Occupation: 1870 in Precinct 4, Hunt County, Texas; Farmer

John A. Schenck and Frances M. Weatherly had the following children:

    i. LAURA VICTORIA[6] SCHENCK was born on 15 Aug 1860 in Lone Oak, Hunt County, Texas. She died on 07 Nov 1898 in Lone Oak, Hunt County, Texas. She married WILLIAM LEMIAL HARRISON. He was born on 22 Sep 1856 in Georgia. He died on 10 Nov 1922 in Lone Oak, Hunt County, Texas.

        More About Laura Victoria Schenck:
        Burial: Lone Oak Cemetery, Hunt County, Texas

    ii. SARAH M. SCHENCK was born on 24 Jan 1862 in Hunt County, Texas. She died on 12 May 1942 in Greenville, Hunt County, Texas. She married J. M. Barnes on 02 Mar 1882 in Hunt County, Texas. He was born on 13 May 1850. He died on 24 May 1895 in Hunt County, Texas.

        More About Sarah M. Schenck:
        Burial: 13 May 1942 in Lone Oak Cemetery, Hunt County, Texas

        Notes for Sarah M. Schenck:
        Headstone has January 24, 1862 for date of birth. Death certificate has January 24, 1863 for date of birth.

    iii. WILLIAM J. SCHENCK was born on 02 Apr 1865 in Hunt County, Texas. He died on 10 Dec 1922 in Hunt County, Texas. He married (1) LIZZIE E. BYRD on 18 May 1890 in Hunt County, Texas. She was born on 18 Feb 1869. She died on 05 Apr 1894 in Hunt County, Texas. He married (2) NOLLIE GORMAN on 06 Feb 1896 in Hunt County, Texas. She was born on 29 Dec 1869 in Texas. She died on 07 Apr 1943 in Hunt County, Texas.

        More About William J. Schenck:
        Burial: Lone Oak Cemetery, Hunt County, Texas
        Occupation: 1900 in Lone Oak, Hunt County, Texas; Merchant
        Occupation: 1910 in Lone Oak, Hunt County, Texas; Hardware Merchant

    iv. MARY F. SCHENCK was born on 17 Sep 1868 in Hunt County, Texas. She died on 21 Jan 1893 in Hunt County, Texas. She married John Neal White on 08 Aug 1888 in Hunt County, Texas. He was born in 1867 in Louisiana. He died in 1941 in Lone Oak, Texas.

        More About Mary F. Schenck:
        Burial: Hall Cemetery, Lone Oak, Texas

12.   **WILLIAM SANFORD**[5] **WEATHERLY** (William W.[4], Isaac[3], William[2], Thomas[1]) was born on 12 Mar 1812 in Clarke County, Georgia. He died on 08 Dec 1889 in Athens, Clarke County, Georgia. He married Elizabeth Nance on 30 Aug 1838 in Randolph County, Georgia. She was born on 01 Jan 1820 in Georgia. She died on 01 May 1890 in Athens, Georgia.

More About William Sanford Weatherly:
Burial: Oconee Hill Cemetery, Athens, Clarke County, Georgia
Occupation: 1850 in Athens, Clarke County, Georgia; Harness Maker
Occupation: 1860 in Athens, Clarke County, Georgia; Mechanic
Occupation: 1880 in Buck Branch, Clarke County, Georgia; Farmer

More About Elizabeth Nance:
Burial: Oconee Hill Cemetery, Athens, Clarke County, Georgia

Notes for Elizabeth Nance:
"Elizabeth Nance Wife of W.S. Weatherly" on her head stone.

William Sanford Weatherly and Elizabeth Nance had the following children:

i.　　SARAH F.[6] WEATHERLY was born in 1836 in Clarke County, Georgia. She married S. C. Rose on 26 Sep 1850 in Clarke County, Georgia.

ii.　　JOSEPH M. WEATHERLY was born on 21 Jan 1837 in Clarke County, Georgia. He died on 18 Dec 1916 in Athens, Clarke County, Georgia. He married MARY A. (UNKNOWN). She was born on 22 Feb 1842 in South Carolina. She died on 07 Feb 1915 in Athens, Clarke County, Georgia.

　　　More About Joseph M. Weatherly:
　　　Burial: Oconee Hill Cemetery, Athens, Clarke County, Georgia

iii.　　JOHN SANFORD WEATHERLY was born on 14 Apr 1838 in Clarke County, Georgia. He died on 28 Apr 1903 in Jefferson, Georgia. He married Rhoda Elizabeth Cheney on 18 Mar 1861 in Greene County, Georgia. She was born on 26 Nov 1843 in Georgia. She died on 27 Dec 1923 in Jefferson, Georgia.

iv.　　MARY E. WEATHERLY was born in 1843 in Clarke County, Georgia. She died in 1916 in Athens, Clarke County, Georgia. She married Hugh Robertson Bernard on 22 Aug 1867 in Clarke County, Georgia. He was born in 1843. He died in 1916 in Athens, Clarke County, Georgia.

　　　More About Mary E. Weatherly:
　　　Burial: Oconee Hill Cemetery, Athens, Clarke County, Georgia

v.　　ROSE WEATHERLY was born in 1845 in Clarke County, Georgia. She married (UNKNOWN) WYATT.

vi.　　WILLIAM A. WEATHERLY was born in Aug 1850 in Clarke County, Georgia. He married LUCY (UNKNOWN). She was born in Dec 1855 in Georgia.

vii.　　CHARLES NANCE WEATHERLY was born on 18 Apr 1862 in Clarke County, Georgia. He died on 19 Aug 1929 in Athens, Clarke County, Georgia. He married Jenny Springs Price on 06 Jan 1884 in Athens, Georgia. She was born on 11 Apr 1862 in Orangeburg, South Carolina. She died on 10 Oct 1931 in Athens, Clarke County, Georgia.

　　　More About Charles Nance Weatherly:

Burial: Oconee Hill Cemetery, Athens, Clarke County, Georgia
Occupation: 1880 in Buck Branch, Clarke County, Georgia; Farmer

13.   JOSEPH JUDGE[5] WEATHERLY (William W.[4], Isaac[3], William[2], Thomas[1]) was born on 18 Feb 1813 in Clarke County, Georgia. He died on 24 Mar 1888 in Benton County, Tennessee. He married (1) VIRGINIA VINSON WOODSON on 31 Jan 1839 in Henry County, Tennessee. She was born on 04 Apr 1824 in Tennessee. She died on 30 Nov 1857. He married (2) MARGARET M. HUGHES on 10 Nov 1858 in Henry County, Tennessee. She was born about 1826 in North Carolina. She died on 27 Jan 1897 in Benton County, Tennessee.

More About Joseph Judge Weatherly:
Burial: Flatwoods Methodist Cemetery, Camden, Benton County,
Tennessee
Living In: 1860 Athens Township, Benton County, Tennessee
Occupation: 1870 in District 10, Benton County, Tennessee; Farmer
Occupation: 1880 in District 10, Benton County, Tennessee; Farmer
Property: 1870 in Benton County, Tennessee; 100 Acres Improved and 200 Acres Unimproved

Joseph Judge Weatherly and Virginia Vinson Woodson had the following children:

    i.   ELIZABETH J.[6] WEATHERLY was born in 1840. She married William N. Robbins on 01 Dec 1858.

    ii.   WILMOTH WEATHERLY was born in 1843.

    iii.   RICHARD WILLIAM WEATHERLY was born on 12 Mar 1846. He died on 10 Jan 1933 in Hamburg, Arkansas. He married LIZZIE HUDSON. He married (2) LOUELLA WITT HOLLAND on 06 Feb 1890. She was born on 16 Nov 1869. She died on 22 May 1943 in Hamburg, Arkansas. He married JANE CLARK.

        More About Richard William Weatherly: Burial:
        Mt. Zion Cemetery, Hamburg, Arkansas

    iv.   MARY WEATHERLY was born in 1848.

    v.   ELLA VIRGINIA WEATHERLY was born on 19 Aug 1857. She died on 18 Jul 1921. She married C. K. HUDSON.

More About Margaret M. Hughes:
Burial: Flatwoods Methodist Cemetery, Camden, Benton County, Tennessee

Joseph Judge Weatherly and Margaret M. Hughes had the following children:

    vi.   MARY ELLEN WEATHERLY was born in 1860. She died on 26 Jul 1880. She married John W. Bell in 1879.

    vii.   JAMES G. WEATHERLY was born in 1863.

    viii.   WALTER B. WEATHERLY was born on 18 Apr 1864. He died on 12 Jul 1873.

    ix.   JOSEPH WEATHERLY was born in 1866.

14.   STATIRAH ELIZABETH[5] WEATHERLY (William W.[4], Isaac[3], William[2], Thomas[1]) was born on 05 Oct 1815 in Clarke County, Georgia. She died on 21 Sep 1897 in Catoosa County, Georgia. She

married William Madison Nance, son of John Nance and Elizabeth Ryan on 19 Jun 1835 in Clarke County, Georgia. He was born on 18 Dec 1809 in Georgia. He died on 11 Apr 1863 in Catoosa County, Georgia.

More About Statirah Elizabeth Weatherly:
Burial: Lee's Chapel Methodist Church Cemetery, Catoosa County, Georgia
Living In: 1870 With five of her children in Catoosa, Catoosa County, Georgia.
Living In: 1880 With three of her children in Catoosa, Catoosa County, Georgia

Notes for Statirah Elizabeth Weatherly:
Spelling of her first name is from her headstone. Birth and death dates are from her headstone.

More About William Madison Nance:
Burial: Lee's Chapel Methodist Church Cemetery, Catoosa County, Georgia
Occupation: 1850 in Murray County, Georgia; Farmer
Occupation: 1860 in Catoosa County, Georgia; Farmer
Property: 1850 in Murray County, Georgia; 70 Acres Improved and 250 Acres Unimproved

Notes for William Madison Nance:
Birth and death dates are from his head stone.

William Madison Nance and Statirah Elizabeth Weatherly had the following children:

    i. MARY E.[6] NANCE was born in 1840 in Georgia. She died in 1883 in Bradley County, Tennessee. She married James Harrison Wilhoit on 27 Feb 1866 in Catoosa County, Georgia. He was born in 1827. He died in 1891 in Bradley County, Tennessee.

    More About Mary E. Nance:
    Burial: Wesleyann Cemetery, Apison, Tennessee

    ii.   SARAH E. NANCE was born in 1842 in Georgia. She died on 24 Mar 1920 in Chattanooga, Tennessee. She married Joseph Emmanuel Stockburger, son of Jacob Stockburger and Nancy (unknown) on 30 Nov 1865 in Catoosa County, Georgia. He was born on 05 Mar 1843. He died on 27 Jan 1889 in Whitfield County, Georgia.

    More About Sarah E. Nance:
    Burial: Concord Baptist Cemetery, Chattanooga, Tennessee

    iii.   CASANDRA MATILDA NANCE was born on 03 Mar 1848 in Georgia. She died on 28 Jun 1916 in Whitfield County, Georgia. She married Augustus Edward Stockburger, son of Jacob Stockburger and Nancy (unknown) on 31 May 1871 in Catoosa County, Georgia. He was born on 08 Mar 1845. He died on 18 Aug 1932 in Whitfield County, Georgia.

    More About Casandra Matilda Nance:
    Burial: Mount Olivet, Cohutta, Georgia
    Living In: 1870 With her mother in Catoosa, Catoosa County, Georgia

    iv.   JAMES M. NANCE was born on 15 Oct 1849 in Murray County, Georgia. He died on 18 Jul 1925 in Lone Oak, Hunt County, Texas. He married Nancy L. Rawley, daughter of Darius Rawley and Purlina McCraw on 28 Dec 1873 in Lone Oak, Texas. She was born on 01 Jan 1855 in Kentucky. She died on 10 Oct 1929 in Lone Oak, Hunt County, Texas.

More About James M. Nance:
b: 15 Oct 1849
Burial: Lone Oak Cemetery, Hunt County, Texas
Occupation: 1870 in Catoosa, Catoosa County, Georgia; Farmer

v.   JOHN ASBURY NANCE was born on 31 May 1851 in Georgia. He died on 02 Nov 1904 in Catoosa County, Georgia.

More About John Asbury Nance:
Living In: 1880 With his mother in Catoosa, Catoosa County, Georgia.
Occupation: 1880 in Catoosa, Catoosa County, Georgia; Farm Laborer

vi.   WILLIAM OSBORN NANCE was born on 30 Jan 1853 in Georgia. He died on 18 Apr 1924 in Catoosa County, Georgia. He married Virginia Elizabeth Scott, daughter of William Scott and Elizabeth Blankbickler on 20 Nov 1879. She was born on 07 Sep 1858 in Tennessee. She died on 27 Apr 1938 in Catoosa County, Georgia.

More About William Osborn Nance:
Burial: Smith Chapel Cemetery, Catoosa County, Georgia
Living In: 1880 William and his wife are living with his mother in Catoosa, Catoosa County, Georgia
Occupation: 1880 in Catoosa, Catoosa County, Georgia; Farm Laborer

vii.   ROBERT WESLEY NANCE was born on 14 Mar 1856 in Georgia. He died on 04 Feb 1905 in Catoosa County, Georgia. He married Mary Emma Scott, daughter of Shalem Scott and Ann Bennett on 16 Jan 1881 in Hunt County, Texas. She was born on 09 Aug 1864 in Texas. She died on 21 Jul 1938 in Catoosa County, Georgia.

More About Robert Wesley Nance:
Burial: Smith Chapel Cemetery, Catoosa County, Georgia

15.   ISAAC C.[5] WEATHERLY (William W.[4], Isaac[3], William[2], Thomas[1]) was born on 15 Jun 1817 in Clarke County, Georgia. He died on 15 Aug 1887 in Lone Oak, Hunt County, Texas. He married Rachael A. Crabb, daughter of James Burton Crabb and Rachel Jones on 14 Feb 1839 in Henry County, Georgia. She was born on 22 Dec 1822 in Columbia County, Georgia. She died on 08 Sep 1896 in Lone Oak, Hunt County, Texas.

More About Isaac C. Weatherly:
Burial: Lone Oak Cemetery, Lone Oak, Hunt County, Texas
Occupation: 1850 in Militia District 848, Paulding County, Georgia; Tailor
Occupation: 1860 in Division 1, Cherokee County, Alabama; Farmer
Occupation: 1880 in Precinct 4, Hunt County, Texas; Farmer

More About Rachael A. Crabb:
Burial: Lone Oak Cemetery, Lone Oak, Hunt County, Texas

Isaac C. Weatherly and Rachael A. Crabb had the following children:

  i. BENJAMIN FRANKLIN[6] WEATHERLY was born on 10 Dec 1839 in Cedartown, Georgia. He died on 10 Mar 1926 in Greeneville, Texas.

    More About Benjamin Franklin Weatherly:
    Burial: Lone Oak Cemetery, Lone Oak, Hunt County, Texas
    Occupation: Farmer
    Occupation: Fire Insurance salesman
    Occupation: School Teacher
    Military Service: Bet. 04 Mar 1862-03 May 1865; Company A, First Georgia Cavalry, C. S. A.

    Notes for Benjamin Franklin Weatherly:
    Paroled at Charlotte, North Carolina on May 3, 1865. 1st Georgia Cavalry was surrendered on April 26, 1865 by order of General Johnston C.S.A. Benjamin Weatherly Never Married.

26. ii. STATIRA OLIVIA WEATHERLY was born on 03 Jul 1840 in Cedartown, Polk County, Georgia. She died on 28 Mar 1914 in Dallas, Dallas County, Texas. She married Elihu Cason, son of Benjamin Cason and Sarah (unknown) on 02 Nov 1859 in Polk County, Georgia. He was born in 1825 in South Carolina. He died on 13 Apr 1897 in Dallas, Texas.

27. iii. ELIZABETH OCTAVIA WEATHERLY was born on 29 May 1843 in Georgia. She died on 11 Sep 1891 in Lone Oak, Hunt County, Texas. She married Edward Weeden before 1866. He was born on 14 May 1833 in Maryland. He died on 02 Jun 1908 in Lone Oak, Hunt County, Texas.

28. iv. ORVIN JOSEPH BURTON WEATHERLY was born on 07 Sep 1844 in Alabama. He died on 05 Sep 1918 in Lone Oak, Texas. He married Sarah Penelope Sheppard, daughter of Henry Sheppard and Mary Holton on 29 Dec 1873 in Hunt County, Texas. She was born on 06 Dec 1846 in Georgia. She died on 14 Dec 1912 in Lone Oak, Texas.

  v. ONY ALBINA WEATHERLY was born on 07 Nov 1845 in Alabama. She died on 03 Mar 1878 in Texas. She married Thomas Jefferson Worthy on 04 May 1876 in Texas. He was born in 1846 in Georgia. He died on 27 Dec 1883 in Winnsboro, Texas.

29. vi. FRANCIS A. WEATHERLY was born on 22 Jun 1848 in Alabama. He died in 1908 in Lone Oak, Hunt County, Texas. He married Tennie Hunt on 31 Dec 1873. She was born in 1853. She died in 1894 in Lone Oak, Hunt County, Texas.

  vii. ANNA WEATHERLY was born on 29 Nov 1849 in Alabama. She married Thomas B. Hubbard on 28 Apr 1868 in Polk County, Georgia. He was born in Oct 1846 in Paulding County, Georgia. He died in 1914 in Rockmart, Georgia.

  viii. DAVID C. WEATHERLY was born on 24 Jun 1851 in Georgia. He died on 30 Jan 1871 in Texas.

30. ix. CARRIE WEATHERLY was born on 10 Mar 1853 in Cedertown, Georgia. She died on 16 Feb 1919 in Lone Oak, Hunt County, Texas. She married Andrew Alexander Payne, son of Nathan Payne and Mary Elizabeth Glass on 16 Mar 1876 in Lone Oak, Hunt County, Texas. He was born on 09 May 1848 in Barren County,

Kentucky. He died on 07 Oct 1920 in Lone Oak, Hunt County, Texas.

31.   x. ROBERT LEON WEATHERLY was born on 20 Dec 1855 in Georgia. He died on 18 Apr 1943 in Hunt County, Texas. He married Mary Ann Hunt on 30 Sep 1879 in Lone Oak, Texas. She was born on 15 Feb 1861 in Hooker Ridge, Texas. She died on 17 Jul 1960 in Hunt County, Texas.

32.   xi. LILLIAN WEATHERLY was born on 06 Oct 1858 in Cedertown, Georgia. She died on 09 Jul 1938 in Lone Oak, Hunt County, Texas. She married Thomas Jefferson Worthy on 19 Dec 1878 in Hunt County, Texas. He was born in 1846 in Georgia. He died on 27 Dec 1883 in Winnsboro, Texas.

     xii. JESSE DANIEL WEATHERLY was born on 30 May 1860 in Alabama. He died on 09 Jun 1878 in Hunt County, Texas.

33.   xiii. THOMAS MADISON WEATHERLY was born on 28 Jan 1864 in Georgia. He died on 04 Apr 1935 in Lone Oak, Hunt County, Texas. He married Mae Elizabeth Cole, daughter of William Cole and Louisa Weeden on 03 Nov 1886 in Lone Oak, Texas. She was born on 11 Oct 1868 in Texas. She died on 15 Sep 1951 in Lone Oak, Hunt County, Texas.

Generation 6

16. **MARY FRANCIS**[6] **WEATHERLY** (Augustus Graham[5], William W.[4], Isaac[3], William[2], Thomas[1]) was born on 19 Sep 1848 in Paulding County, Georgia. She died on 10 Apr 1915 in Denton, Texas. She married William Payne, son of Nathan Payne and Mary Elizabeth Glass on 06 Dec 1865 in Hunt County, Texas. He was born on 06 Nov 1842 in Barren County, Kentucky. He died on 02 Nov 1909 in Denton, Texas.

More About Mary Francis Weatherly:
Burial: Odd Fellows Cemetery, Denton, Texas
Living In: 1910 Denton, Denrton County, Texas

Notes for Mary Francis Weatherly:
Francis is the correct spelling for Mary's middle name.

More About William Payne:
Burial: Odd Fellows Cemetery, Denton, Texas
Living In: 1850 Barren County, Kentucky
Living In: 1860 Hunt County, Texas
Occupation: 1870 in Precinct 4, Hunt County, Texas; Farmer
Occupation: 1880 in Precinct 4, Hunt County, Texas; Farmer
Occupation: 1900 in Whitewright, Grayson County, Texas; Landlord
Occupation: Mayor of Whitewright, Texas
Military Service: Soldier C.S.A.

Notes for William Payne:
Will dated September 9, 1902.
Will filed November 4, 1909.
Application for Probate of Will, County Court of Denton County, Texas, January term 1910.

William Payne and Mary Francis Weatherly had the following children:

i. FLORA BELLE[7] PAYNE was born on 15 Dec 1868 in Lone Oak, Texas. She died on 30 Dec 1938 in Sherman, Texas. She married (1) CHARLES EDWARD SAVAGE, son of Edward William Savage and Martha Jane Trussell on 15 Feb 1893 in Grayson County, Texas. He was born on 10 Jan 1867 in Grenada, Mississippi. He died on 01 Mar 1919 in Sherman, Texas. She married (2) WILLIAM HICKS BRAY, son of James Bray and Mary Wilson on 11 Sep 1934 in Clay County, Texas. He was born on 08 Jan 1868 in Texas. He died on 14 May 1941 in Lubbock, Texas.

More About Flora Belle Payne:
Burial: 31 Dec 1938 in West Hill Cemetery, Grayson County,
Texas Cause Of Death: Coronary Occlusion
Living In: 1920 Living with her minor children, Nina Lea and William, as a widow in Sherman, Grayson County, Texas
Living In: 1930 Living with her daughter, Nina Lea, and her husband in Okemah, Okfuskee County, Oklahoma

Notes for Flora Belle Payne:
Living with Al Bryan and family in Okemah, Oklahoma in 1930.

ii. MARY ELIZABETH PAYNE was born on 04 Nov 1866 in Lone Oak, Texas. She died on 23 Jan 1957 in University Park, Dallas County, Texas. She married Charles W. Melson on 29 Feb 1888 in Hunt County, Texas. He was born on 06 Oct 1860 in Missouri. He died on 21 Sep 1925 in Floydada, Floyd County, Texas.

More About Mary Elizabeth Payne:
Burial: Odd Fellows Cemetery, Denton, Denton County, Texas
Living In: 1910 Living with her daughters, Mary and Addie, in Denton, Denton County, Texas
Living In: 1920 Living with her daughters, Mary and Addie, in Denton, Denton County, Texas
Living In: 1940 Living with her daughter, Addie, in Dallas, Dallas County, Texas.

iii. WILLIAM EMMET PAYNE was born on 10 Feb 1872 in Texas. He died on 07 Feb 1920 in Gainsville, Texas. He married HATTIE ANN BURT. She was born on 22 Dec 1896 in Arkansas. She died on 25 Aug 1976 in Plainview, Hale County, Texas.

More About William Emmet Payne:
Living In: 1900 Living with his parents in Whitewright, Grayson County, Texas.
Living In: 1910 Township 6, Bryan County, Oklahoma
Living In: 03 Jan 1920 With his wife and sons in Kemp, Bryan County, Oklahoma.
Occupation: 1900 in Whitewright, Grayson County, Texas; Day Laborer

Notes for William Emmet Payne:
1900 Census gives July 1872 as birthdate.

iv. LESLIE NEWTON PAYNE was born on 14 Jun 1874 in Texas. He died on 16 Apr 1932 in Gainesville, Cooke County, Texas. He married Lela Belle Biffle, daughter of J. T. Biffle and Mary Jane Brown on 01 May 1901 in Cooke County, Texas. She was born on 05 Oct 1882 in Myra, Cooke County, Texas. She died on 23 Dec 1948 in Myra, Cooke County, Texas.

More About Leslie Newton Payne:
Burial: 18 Apr 1932 in Reed Cemetery, Myra, Cooke County, Texas
Living In: 1900 Living with his parents in Whitewright, Grayson County, Texas.
Occupation: 1900 in Whitewright, Grayson County, Texas; Fire Insurance Agent
Occupation: 1910 in El Paso, El Paso county, Texas; Local Manager for Oil Company
Occupation: 1920 in San Antonio, Bexar County, Texas; Commercial Traveler for Tires
Occupation: 1930 in Fort Worth, Tarrant County, Texas; Salesman for Oil Supply Company

v.   METTIE KATHRYN PAYNE was born on 04 Dec 1877 in Texas. She died on 14 Apr 1947 in Fort Worth, Tarrant County, Texas. She married Marion Pace, son of W. A. Pace and Sarah Hawkins after 30 May 1912. He was born on 11 Jul 1852 in Indiana. He died on 17 Jul 1930 in Cleburne, Johnson County, Texas.

More About Mettie Kathryn Payne:
Burial: 16 Apr 1947 in Cleburne Memorial Cemetery, Cleburne, Johnson County, Texas
Living In: 1910 Living with her mother in Denton, Denton County, Texas.

vi.   FRANCES EDITH PAYNE was born on 18 Dec 1880 in Lone Oak, Texas. She died on 04 Jan 1957 in University Park, Dallas County, Texas. She married JOSEPH NELSON FENDER. He was born on 02 Jan 1877 in Kaufman County, Texas. He died on 28 Nov 1967 in Dallas, Dallas County, Texas.

More About Frances Edith Payne:
Burial: College Mound Cemetery, Terrell, Kaufman County, Texas
Living In: 1910 Living with her mother in Denton, Denton County, Texas.

vii.   GRAHAM LEWIS PAYNE was born on 09 Mar 1883 in Texas. He died on 14 Apr 1951 in Dallas, Dallas County, Texas. He married MADELEINE ROSE MADDEN. She was born on 24 Nov 1892 in Texas. She died on 12 May 1976 in Dallas, Dallas County, Texas.

More About Graham Lewis Payne:
Burial: Odd Fellows Cemetery, Denton, Denton County, Texas Cause Of Death: Acute Myocardial Infarction
Occupation: 1910 in Fort Worth, Tarrant County, Texas; Manager of Tailoring Company
Occupation: 1920 in Dallas, Dallas County, Texas; Shoe Company Salesman
Occupation: 1930 in Dallas, Dallas County, Texas; Jobber at Wholesale House
Occupation: 1940 in Preston Hollow, Dallas County, Texas; Manufacturer with Underwear Factory
Occupation: 1951 in Dallas, Dallas County, Texas; Proprietor of Garment Factory

Notes   for   Graham   Lewis
Payne: No Issue.

17.   SARAH ELIZABETH[6] WEATHERLY (Augustus Graham[5], William W.[4], Isaac[3], William[2], Thomas[1]) was

born on 06 Feb 1850 in Cedartown, Polk County, Georgia. She died on 02 Feb 1942 in Victoria, Victoria County, Texas. She married Robert Pinkney Rawley, son of Darius Rawley and Purlina McCraw on 14 Feb 1867 in Lone Oak, Hunt County, Texas. He was born on 30 May 1841 in Reedsville, North Carolina. He died on 18 Jan 1915 in Victoria, Texas.

More About Sarah Elizabeth Weatherly:
Burial: 03 Feb 1942 in Evergreen Cemetery, Victoria, Victoria County, Texas
Living In: 1940 With her grandson, Rawley W. Ward, and his family in Victoria, Victoria County, Texas.

More About Robert Pinkney Rawley:
Burial: 19 Jan 1915 in Evergreen Cemetery, Victoria, Victoria County, Texas
Occupation: 1870 in Precinct 4, Hunt County, Texas; Home Carpenter
Occupation: 1880 in Precinct 4, Hunt County, Texas; Merchant
Occupation: 1900 in Justice Precinct 1, Victoria County, Texas; Carpenter
Occupation: 1910 in Justice Precinct 1, Victoria County, Texas; Retired
Military Service: 15 Dec 1861 in Enlisted in Greenville, Hunt County, Texas; Company D, 22nd Texas Cavalry, C.S.A. (promoted to Corporal)

Notes for Robert Pinkney
Rawley: ROBERT P. RAWLEY
DIED THIS MORNING
(Victoria Advocate - January 18, 1915)

Robert Pinkney Rawley, aged 74 years, died in this city at the home of his daughter, Mrs. Dr. W. L. Ward, this morning, Monday, January 18, 1915, at 9:30 o'clock. Mr. Rawley had been in declining health for nearly a year, and was confined to his bed for the past six months.

Mr. Rawley was born in Reedsville, North Carolina, May 30, 1841. He was a member of one of the most prominent families of his native state, his father being the owner of a large plantation. He removed to Kentucky the latter part of the '50's, and a short time later came to Texas.

For two years Mr. Rawley was a member of the state ranger force, serving in the capacity of a volunteer and achieving distinction for his bravery. At the outbreak of the Civil War he joined the Thirteenth Texas Cavalry, Maverick's Battalion, and became an orderly under General Dick Taylor, the noted commander of the Trans-Mississippi Department of the Confederacy. He participated in many of the most important battles of the war, and was repeatedly promoted for his gallantry.

Mr. Rawley was married February 14, 1867, to Miss Elizebath (sic) Weathley (sic), daughter of the late Mr. & Mrs. A. J. Weatherly, of Hunt County, where he was engaged in the mercantile business for a number of years. He and Mrs. Rawley removed to Victoria in 1894.

Surviving the decedent are his widow and two children, Mrs. W. L. Ward, of this city, and L. W. Rawley, of Bakersfield, California. He is also survived by two sisters, Mrs. T. S. Weatherly and Mrs. James Nance, of Lone Oak, Hunt County.

The funeral will take place from the Ward residence tomorrow (Tuesday) afternoon at 4:00 o'clock. The Rev. W. M. Crutchfield, pastor of the Victoria Methodist Church, will officiate, and the interment will be made in the Evergreen Cemetery. M. H. Williams, Dr. D. H. Braman, Roy Stubblefield, Albert Schneider, A. K. Wilson, and Dr. Fred B. Shields will serve as pall bearers.

Robert Pinkney Rawley and Sarah Elizabeth Weatherly had the following children:

    i. CORRA IDELL [7] RAWLEY was born on 01 Sep 1868 in Lone Oak, Hunt County, Texas. She died on 13 Nov 1931 in Victoria, Texas. She married William Levi Ward, son of

Mathias Ward and Malinda Moore on 27 Nov 1888 in McGregor, Texas. He was born on 09 Jul 1852 in Blount County, Alabama. He died on 27 Dec 1938 in Victoria, Texas.

More About Corra Idell Rawley:
Burial: 14 Nov 1931 in Evergreen Cemetery, Victoria, Victoria County, Texas

ii.   LUTHER WILLIAM RAWLEY was born on 28 Oct 1871 in Lone Oak, Texas. He died on 12 Sep 1951 in Kern County, California. He married Maude E. Morgan on 01 Jan 1907 in Bakersfield, California. She was born on 21 Oct 1880. She died on 05 Nov 1962 in Bakersfield, Kern County, California.

More About Luther William Rawley:
Burial: Union Cemetery, Bakersfield, Kern County, California
Military Service: Spanish American War; Corporal in 1st Washington Infantry

18.   **JAMES A.**[6] **WEATHERLY** (Augustus Graham[5], William W.[4], Isaac[3], William[2], Thomas[1]) was born on 20 Sep 1855 in Paulding County, Georgia. He died on 07 Apr 1899 in Greeneville, Texas. He married Edna Paralee Horn on 04 Nov 1877 in Hunt County, Texas. She was born on 15 Apr 1858 in Texas. She died on 06 Apr 1910 in Greeneville, Texas.

More About James A. Weatherly:
Burial: East Mount Cemetery, Greeneville, Hunt County, Texas
Occupation: 1880 in Precinct 4, Hunt County, Texas; Farmer

More About Edna Paralee Horn:
Burial: East Mount Cemetery, Greeneville, Hunt County, Texas
Occupation: 1900 in Greenville, Hunt County, Texas; Land Lady

James A. Weatherly and Edna Paralee Horn had the following children:

i. WILLIAM A.[7] WEATHERLY was born on 21 May 1883 in Texas. He died on 02 Nov 1970 in Ventura County, California.

More About William A. Weatherly:
Burial: Ivy Lawn Memorial Park, Ventura, Ventura County, California

ii.   BETTIE WEATHERLY was born on 01 Feb 1885 in Texas. She married John J. Harris on 20 Jan 1909 in Lone Oak, Texas.

iii.   ANNIE WEATHERLY was born in Sep 1887 in Texas.

iv.   MARY EDNA WEATHERLY was born in Feb 1889 in Texas.

v.   JAMES ROY WEATHERLY was born on 04 Aug 1897 in Texas. He died on 25 Mar 1965 in Ventura County, California.

More About James Roy Weatherly:
Burial: Ivy Lawn Memorial Park, Ventura, Ventura County, California

vi.   JIMMIE WEATHERLY was born in Oct 1898 in Texas.

19. **A. Matilda[6] Weatherly** (Augustus Graham[5], William W.[4], Isaac[3], William[2], Thomas[1]) was born in 1858 in Texas. She died after 15 Apr 1910. She married T. H. Green on 22 Nov 1876 in Hunt County, Texas. He was born about 1850 in South Carolina. He died before 15 Apr 1910.

More About A. Matilda Weatherly:
Living In: 1910 Living as a widow with her daughter, Bennie, and her family in Pine Bluff, Jefferson County, Arkansas.

T. H. Green and A. Matilda Weatherly had the following children:

    i.   V.[7] Green was born about 1877 in Texas.

    ii.   Bernice Green was born about 1878 in Texas. She died after 1950. She married Samuel C. Alexander. He was born about 1859 in North Carolina. He died before 12 Apr 1940.

        More About Bernice Green:
        Occupation: 1940 in Pine Bluff, Jefferson County, Arkansas; Land Lady at Boarding House
        Occupation: 1951 in Fayetteville, Arkansas; Housemother at Chi Omega

20. **Georgia Virginia[6] Weatherly** (Augustus Graham[5], William W.[4], Isaac[3], William[2], Thomas[1]) was born on 08 Jun 1863 in Lone Oak, Texas. She died on 25 Jul 1919 in Celeste, Hunt County, Texas. She married Auburn Monroe Neal, son of Joseph James Neal and Martha Glover Garrett on 13 Oct 1880 in Lone Oak, Texas. He was born on 15 Aug 1859 in Callaway County, Missouri. He died on 20 Nov 1933 in Zephyr, Brown County, Texas.

More About Georgia Virginia Weatherly:
Burial: 27 Jul 1919 in Queen City Cemetery, Queen City, Cass County, Texas

More About Auburn Monroe Neal:
Burial: 21 Nov 1933 in Zephyr Cemetery, Zephyr, Brown County, Texas
Living In: 1880 With his parents in Precinct 4, Hunt County, Texas.
Living In: 1920 With his daughter, Bessie, and her family in Celeste, Hunt County, Texas.
Occupation: 1880 in Precinct 4, Hunt County, Texas; Farm Worker
Occupation: 1900 in Queen Cities, Cass County, Texas; Physician
Occupation: 1920 in Celeste, Hunt County, Texas; Medical Physician

Auburn Monroe Neal and Georgia Virginia Weatherly had the following children:

    i.   Walter Monroe[7] Neal was born on 28 Oct 1881 in Lone Oak, Texas. He died on 28 Aug 1907 in Queen City, Cass County, Texas. He married Vera Gertrude Williams, daughter of William Williams and Mary (unknown) on 07 Jun 1903 in Vivian, Louisiana. She was born on 12 Jun 1886 in Vivian, Louisiana.

        More About Walter Monroe Neal:
        Burial: Queen City Cemetery, Queen City, Cass County, Texas

    ii.   Bessie Mary Neal was born on 29 Nov 1882 in Lone Oak, Texas. She died on 10 Jun 1961 in Greenville, Hunt County, Texas. She married Silas Victor Baker, son of John Baker and Artie Waggoner on 15 Feb 1905 in Queen City, Texas. He was born on 26 Jun 1878 in Franklin, Arkansas. He died on 06 May 1967 in Greenville, Hunt County, Texas.

More About Bessie Mary Neal:
Burial: 11 Jun 1961 in East Mount Cemetery, Greenville, Hunt County, Texas

    iii.   E. C. NEAL was born on 10 Apr 1886 in Hunt County, Texas. E. C. died on 13 Sep 1888 in Hunt County, Texas.

    iv.   NINNIA G. NEAL was born on 10 Apr 1892. She died on 23 Apr 1895.

    v.   GORDON GARRETT NEAL was born on 29 Sep 1899 in Campbell, Texas. He died in Mar 1961 in Palo Alto, California. He married ETHYL (UNKNOWN). He married (2) KATHERINE KILLIAN in Feb 1921. He married (3) GAYL GRIFFIS on 01 Oct 1929.

    vi.   WILLIS REAGAN NEAL was born on 30 Aug 1902. He died on 11 Jul 1904.

More About Willis Reagan Neal:
Burial: Queen City Cemetery, Queen City, Cass County, Texas

21.   **TOMMY DELLA**[6] **WEATHERLY** (Augustus Graham[5], William W.[4], Isaac[3], William[2], Thomas[1]) was born on 02 Dec 1868 in Texas. She died on 02 Dec 1961 in Houston, Harris County, Texas. She married (1) **JAMES ANDERSON TAYLOR**, son of S. W. Taylor and Martha A. (unknown) on 23 Sep 1933 in Hunt County, Texas. He was born on 04 Mar 1861 in Alabama. He died on 27 Jun 1956 in Celeste, Hunt County, Texas. She married (2) **RICHARD WARREN** on 18 Dec 1887 in Hunt County, Texas. He was born in 1856 in Mississippi. She married (3) **WILLIAM J. MCNATT** on 16 Dec 1897 in Hunt County, Texas. He was born on 04 Dec 1853 in Tennessee. He died on 10 Apr 1924.

More About Tommy Della Weatherly:
Burial: 05 Dec 1961 in Merit Cemetery, Merit, Hunt County, Texas
Living In: 1930 With W. A. Townsend and his family in Precinct 2, Hunt County, Texas.
Living In: 1940 With James in Celeste, Hunt County, Texas.

Notes for Tommy Della Weatherly:
Greenville Herald Banner, Tue, 5 Dec 1961, page 2, Deaths, Mrs. Della Taylor

Funeral services for Mrs. Della Taylor will be held at 3 p.m. Tuesday in the Sorrells and Sons funeral home chapel. The Rev. Albert Click and the Rev. Bill Pratt of First Baptist Church, Greenville, will officiate.

Burial will be in Merit cemetery. Mrs. Taylor died Saturday at the home of her daughter, Mrs. Moly Mock, Houston.

More About James Anderson Taylor:
Burial: 29 Jun 1956 in Dulaney Cemetery, Hunt County, Texas
Living In: 1940 With Della in Celeste, Hunt County, Texas.

Richard Warren and Tommy Della Weatherly had the following children:

    i.   MARY LEE[7] WARREN was born on 26 Feb 1889 in Texas. She died on 07 Feb 1974 in Houston, Harris County, Texas. She married Floyd Daniel Mock, son of Emmett J. Mock and Blanche Roberts on 13 Oct 1907 in Hunt County, Texas. He was born on 17 Jun 1877 in Hunt County, Texas. He died on 10 Mar 1958 in Houston, Harris County, Texas.

More About Mary lee Warren:
Burial: 09 Feb 1974 in South Park Cemetery, Pearland, Harris County, Texas
Living In: 1900 With her mother and step father in Justice Precinct 2, Hunt County, Texas.

ii.   JOHNIE WARREN was born on 14 Feb 1890 in Texas. He died before 13 Jun 1900.

More About Johnie Warren:
Burial: Hopewell Cemetery, Hunt County, Texas

iii.   THOMAS WARREN was born on 24 Oct 1891 in Greenville, Hunt County, Texas. He died on 14 Mar 1970 in Greenville, Hunt County, Texas. He married LUCILLE M. (UNKNOWN). She was born on 01 Aug 1895 in Arkansas. She died on 28 Oct 1981 in Hunt County, Texas.

More About Thomas Warren:
Burial: 16 Mar 1970 in Memoryland Memorial Park, Greenville, Hunt County, Texas
Living In: 1900 With his mother and step father in Justice Precinct 2, Hunt County, Texas.
Living In: 1910 With his mother and step father in Justice Precinct 2, Hunt County, Texas.
Occupation: Pharmacist
Military Service: Bet. 28 Apr 1918-15 Jun 1919 in Enlisted in Akron, Ohio; American Expeditionary Force, June 20, 1918-June 7, 1919

Notes for Thomas Warren:
From April 28, 1918-May 12, 1918, 165th Depot Brigade. Was in Medical Department 359th Infantry Regiment from May 12, 1918 until discharged on June 15, 1919. Promoted to private first class on November 23, 1918. Awarded Silver Star. Enlisted in Ohio but 165th Depot Brigade and 359th Infantry Regiment were from Texas. The 359th Infantry Regiment was part of the 90th Division in World War One.

More About William J. McNatt:
Burial: Merit Cemetery, Merit, Hunt County, Texas
Occupation: 1900 in Justice Precinct 2, Hunt County, Texas; Practitice of Medicine
Occupation: 1910 in Justice Precinct 2, Hunt County, Texas; Public Physician
Occupation: 1920 in Justice Precinct 2, Hunt County, Texas; Public Doctor

William J. McNatt and Tommy Della Weatherly had the following children:
i.   MYRTLE LEONA[7] MCNATT was born in Mar 1899 in Texas.

ii.   ALTON MCNATT was born on 05 Aug 1903 in Texas. He died on 21 Aug 1925 in Dallas, Dallas County, Texas.

More About Alton McNatt:
Burial: Merit Cemetery, Merit, Hunt County, Texas
Occupation: Carpenter

22.   **ALICE[6] POLLARD** (Sarah C.[5] Weatherly, William W.[4] Weatherly, Isaac[3] Weatherly, William[2] Weatherly, Thomas[1] Weatherly) was born about 1855 in Texas. She died in Lone Oak, Texas. She married Thomas Joseph Bell on 29 Jun 1879 in Hunt County, Texas. He was born in 1854. He died in 1899 in Lone Oak, Texas.

More About Alice Pollard:
Burial: Lone Oak Cemetery, Hunt County, Texas

More About Thomas Joseph Bell:
Burial: Lone Oak Cemetery, Hunt County, Texas

Thomas Joseph Bell and Alice Pollard had the following children:

        i.   IVAN IRELL[7] BELL was born in 1880. He died in 1955.

             More About Ivan Irell Bell:
             Burial: Woodbine Cemetery, Artesia, Eddy County, New Mexico

        ii.   FLOYD BELL.

        iii.   ALMIRA BELL.

        iv.   CLARA C. BELL. She married THOMAS RICHARD HANSON.

        v.   WILLIE ISHAM BELL was born on 16 Mar 1884 in Lone Oak, Texas.

23.   **JAMES RALSTON[6] POLLARD** (Sarah C.[5] Weatherly, William W.[4] Weatherly, Isaac[3] Weatherly, William[2] Weatherly, Thomas[1] Weatherly) was born in Nov 1858 in Texas. He died in 1943 in Lone Oak, Texas. He married Carrie Lee McFadden, daughter of Sam McFadden and Nettie Hardin on 14 Jan 1883 in Rains County, Texas. She was born in Jan 1862 in Texas. She died on 27 Aug 1939 in Lone Oak, Texas.

More About James Ralston Pollard:
Burial: Lone Oak Cemetery, Lone Oak, Hunt County, Texas

More About Carrie Lee McFadden:
Burial: Lone Oak Cemetery, Hunt County, Texas

James Ralston Pollard and Carrie Lee McFadden had the following children:

        i.   EVIE E.[7] POLLARD was born on 02 Dec 1884 in Lone Oak, Texas. She died in Jun 1963 in Lone Oak, Texas. She married ARTHUR MCBRIDE.

             More About Evie E. Pollard:
             Occupation: Saleslady in Dry Goods Store

        ii.   ORVAL ROYSTON POLLARD was born on 06 Apr 1887 in Lone Oak, Texas. He died on 27 Feb 1979 in Wichita Falls, Texas. He married Olivia Corley on 28 Dec 1908. She was born on 08 Mar 1890. She died in Jan 1980.

             More   About   Orval   Royston
             Pollard:
             Occupation: Farmer

      iii.   JAMES W. POLLARD was born on 29 Jul 1894. He died on 16 Jul 1962. He married Emma C. Phillips, daughter of A. T. Phillips and Sarah Woosley on 06 Jun 1925. She was born on 06 Nov 1901. She died on 04 Nov 1994 in Greenville, Texas.

24.   **THOMAS A.**[6] **POLLARD** (Sarah C.[5] Weatherly, William W.[4] Weatherly, Isaac[3] Weatherly, William[2] Weatherly, Thomas[1] Weatherly) was born on 27 Jun 1861 in Lone Oak, Texas. He died on 23 Mar 1937. He married **MOLLIE A. ALLEN**. She was born in 1862 in Louisiana. She died on 23 Mar 1911.

Thomas A. Pollard and Mollie A. Allen had the following children:

      i.   MARVIN[7] POLLARD.

      ii.   JOHN THORNTON POLLARD was born on 16 Jan 1882. He died on 10 May 1963. He married PRUNIE MAE FITZGERALD. She was born on 16 Nov 1884. She died on 17 Apr 1973 in Carrollton, Texas.

25.   **REESE DAVID**[6] **POLLARD** (Sarah C.[5] Weatherly, William W.[4] Weatherly, Isaac[3] Weatherly, William[2] Weatherly, Thomas[1] Weatherly) was born in Sep 1869 in Lone Oak, Texas. He married Jessie Goff in 1893. She was born in Apr 1875 in Texas.

Reese David Pollard and Jessie Goff had the following child:

      i.   CLARA[7] POLLARD was born in Nov 1895.

26.   **STATIRA OLIVIA**[6] **WEATHERLY** (Isaac C.[5], William W.[4], Isaac[3], William[2], Thomas[1]) was born on 03 Jul 1840 in Cedartown, Polk County, Georgia. She died on 28 Mar 1914 in Dallas, Dallas County, Texas. She married Elihu Cason, son of Benjamin Cason and Sarah (unknown) on 02 Nov 1859 in Polk County, Georgia. He was born in 1825 in South Carolina. He died on 13 Apr 1897 in Dallas, Texas.

More About Statira Olivia Weatherly:
Burial: 29 Mar 1914 in Oakland Cemetery, Dallas, Dallas County, Texas

Notes for Statira Olivia Weatherly:
    From the Dallas Morning News of Sunday, March 29th, 1914
Headline "Mrs. Olivia Cason Dies. Dallas Woman Survived by 11 Children, 76 Grandchildren, and 18 Great-grandchildren." Mrs Olivia Cason, aged 73 years, widow of the late Elihu Cason, died at 3:45 yesterday afternoon at the residence of her daughter, Mrs. Ben Lockett Adair, 4703 East Side Ave The funeral will be held from the residence this afternoon at 4:30. Services will be conducted by Rev. J. Frank Smith and burial will be in Greenwood Cemetery (it was later decided that burial would be at Oakland Cemetery). Mrs. Cason was the mother of twelve children, five sons and seven daughters, most of whom reside in Dallas. She is also survived by seventy-six grandchildren and eighteen great-grandchildren. The children surviving are: Luther Cason of Cleburne; Elihu Cason, J.C. Cason, Mrs. S.V. Cruthis, B.F. Cason, Mrs. J.J. Chenault, and Mrs. B.L. Adair of Dallas; and Mrs. G.H. Coyle of New York City Mrs. Cason was born in Cedartown, GA., July 3, 1840 and was married to Elihu Cason in 1858. She had resided in Texas forty-one years and in Dallas seventeen years."

Arrived in Texas about 1873.

More About Elihu Cason:
Burial: Oakland Cemetery, Dallas, Texas
Occupation: 1860; Merchant, Dry Goods and Groceries, in Esam Hill, Georgia

Occupation: Bet. 1865-1870; Grocer in Griffin, Georgia
Occupation: Bet. 1870-1872; Farmer near Rome, Georgia
Occupation: Bet. 1872-1895; Farmer in Collin County, Texas
Military Service: 01 Dec 1862; Enlisted in Company A, 1st Georgia Cavalry, C. S. A.

Elihu Cason and Statira Olivia Weatherly had the following children:

i.   LUTHER[7] CASON.

ii. ELIHU CASON was born on 26 Sep 1861 in Georgia. He died on 19 Sep 1917 in Dallas, Texas. He married SARAH JANE COOK. She was born on 14 Jan 1869 in Kentucky. She died on 17 Jul 1910 in Dallas, Texas.

iii. J. C. CASON.

iv. B. F. CASON.

27. **ELIZABETH OCTAVIA**[6] **WEATHERLY** (Isaac C.[5], William W.[4], Isaac[3], William[2], Thomas[1]) was born on 29 May 1843 in Georgia. She died on 11 Sep 1891 in Lone Oak, Hunt County, Texas. She married Edward Weeden before 1866. He was born on 14 May 1833 in Maryland. He died on 02 Jun 1908 in Lone Oak, Hunt County, Texas.

More About Elizabeth Octavia Weatherly:
Burial: Lone Oak Cemetery, Hunt County, Texas

More About Edward Weeden:
Burial: Lone Oak Cemetery, Hunt County, Texas
Occupation: Farmer
Military Service: Company H, 11th Texas Cavalry, C. S. A.

Edward Weeden and Elizabeth Octavia Weatherly had the following children:

i.   MATTIE[7] WEEDEN was born about 1867 in Texas.

ii. WILLIAM C. WEEDEN was born about 1871 in Texas.

iii. CARRIE WEEDEN was born about 1872 in Texas.

iv. ROBERT A. WEEDEN was born about 1874 in Texas.

v.   OCTAVIA WEEDEN was born about 1876 in Texas.

vi. DANIEL WEEDEN was born about 1878 in Texas.

28. **ORVIN JOSEPH BURTON**[6] **WEATHERLY** (Isaac C.[5], William W.[4], Isaac[3], William[2], Thomas[1]) was born on 07 Sep 1844 in Alabama. He died on 05 Sep 1918 in Lone Oak, Texas. He married Sarah Penelope Sheppard, daughter of Henry Sheppard and Mary Holton on 29 Dec 1873 in Hunt County, Texas. She was born on 06 Dec 1846 in Georgia. She died on 14 Dec 1912 in Lone Oak, Texas.

More About Orvin Joseph Burton Weatherly:
Burial: Lone Oak Cemetery, Lone Oak, Hunt County, Texas
Occupation: Wheelwright
Occupation: Farmer

Military Service: Bet. 04 Mar 1862-Dec 1864 ; Company A, 1st Georgia Cavalry, C. S. A.

Notes for Orvin Joseph Burton Weatherly: GOOD
CITIZEN DIES THURSDAY AFTERNOON
  After 2:40 yesterday afternoon our good friend and neighbor J.B. (Uncle Dick as he was called)
Weatherly after many days lingering illness passed away. For many months he had been in
failing health but recently on return from a visit to Wills Point, he was unable to walk about the
place as has been his custom and for some two weeks he was confined to his room.
  Deceased was born in Georgia in 1844 and came to Texas when a young man. He was married
to Miss Nellie Shepperd of Campbell. To this union was given five children, four girls an one boy.
The girls are all living: Mrs. John Shepherd and Mrs. G. R. Barnett of Lone Oak with whom Mr.
Weatherly had lived the past few years, and Mrs. Long of Hiram and Mrs. Dave Shepperd
of Wichita Falls. The latter arrived on the 5:00 o'clock train Thursday afternoon.
  Two brothers of deceased, Tom M. Weatherly and Ben F. Weatherly and two sisters, Mrs. A.
Payne and Mrs. Lillie Worthy live here. Another brother, R. Weatherly came in Thursday
afternoon from his home at Campbell.
  The funeral se4rvices will be conducted at the Baptist church this (Friday) afternoon. The hour
of the services is undetermined awaiting the arrival of Dave Shepherd from Wichita Falls who is
expected to arrive in Greenville on the noon train.

More About Sarah Penelope Sheppard:
Burial: Lone Oak Cemetery, Hunt County, Texas

Orvin Joseph Burton Weatherly and Sarah Penelope Sheppard had the following children:

> i.   DANA[7] WEATHERLY was born in 1876 in Lone Oak, Hunt County, Texas. He died
> in 1882 in Lone Oak, Hunt County, Texas.

> ii.   DAISY MAE WEATHERLY was born on 23 Oct 1879 in Lone Oak, Hunt County,
> Texas. She died on 22 Sep 1963 in Lone Oak, Hunt County, Texas.

> iii.   WILNA RAY WEATHERLY was born on 14 Aug 1882 in Lone Oak, Hunt
> County, Texas. She died in 1960 in San Antonio, Texas.

> iv.   HATTIE CORNELIUS WEATHERLY was born on 20 Nov 1884 in Lone Oak, Hunt
> County, Texas. She died on 21 Jun 1958 in Corsicana, Texas.

> v.   ETHEL LUCILLE WEATHERLY was born on 28 Aug 1886 in Lone Oak, Hunt County,
> Texas.

29.   FRANCIS A.[6] WEATHERLY (Isaac C.[5], William W.[4], Isaac[3], William[2], Thomas[1]) was born on 22 Jun
1848 in Alabama. He died in 1908 in Lone Oak, Hunt County, Texas. He married Tennie Hunt on
31 Dec 1873. She was born in 1853. She died in 1894 in Lone Oak, Hunt County, Texas.

More About Francis A. Weatherly:
Burial: Lone Oak Cemetery, Lone Oak, Hunt County, Texas

More About Tennie Hunt:
Burial: Lone Oak Cemetery, Lone Oak, Hunt County, Texas

Francis A. Weatherly and Tennie Hunt had the following child:

> i.   LILLIE DALE[7] WEATHERLY was born in 1873 in Lone Oak, Hunt County, Texas. She died
> in 1958 in Lone Oak, Hunt County, Texas. She married John Neal White on 13 May
> 1894 in Lone Oak, Texas. He was born in 1867 in Louisiana. He died in 1941

in Lone Oak, Texas.

More About Lillie Dale Weatherly:
Burial: Lone Oak Cemetery, Hunt County, Texas

30.   CARRIE[6] WEATHERLY (Isaac C.[5], William W.[4], Isaac[3], William[2], Thomas[1]) was born on 10 Mar 1853 in Cedertown, Georgia. She died on 16 Feb 1919 in Lone Oak, Hunt County, Texas. She married Andrew Alexander Payne, son of Nathan Payne and Mary Elizabeth Glass on 16 Mar 1876 in Lone Oak, Hunt County, Texas. He was born on 09 May 1848 in Barren County, Kentucky. He died on 07 Oct 1920 in Lone Oak, Hunt County, Texas.

More About Carrie Weatherly:
Burial: 17 Feb 1919 in Lone Oak Cemetery, Hunt County, Texas

Notes for Carrie Weatherly:
Funeral conducted by Reverend J. A. Roper.

More About Andrew Alexander Payne:
Burial: Lone Oak Cemetery, Hunt County, Texas
Living In: 1870 Living with his parents in Precinct 4, Hunt County, Texas.
Occupation: 1870 in Hunt County, Texas; Farm Labor
Occupation: 1880 in Precinct 4, Hunt County, Texas; Farmer
Occupation: 1900 in Lone Oak, Hunt County, Texas; Farmer
Occupation: 1910 in Lone Oak, Hunt County, Texas; City Mayor
Occupation: Hunt County, Texas; Justice of the Peace

Andrew Alexander Payne and Carrie Weatherly had the following children:

 i. FLORENCE[7] PAYNE was born in Aug 1877 in Texas. She married J. V. NASH.

 ii. ALMA R. PAYNE was born on 20 Jan 1879 in Lone Oak, Texas. She died on 26 Feb 1941 in Lone Oak, Hunt County, Texas. She married (1) FRANK N. BRYAN on 12 Jun 1895 in Lone Oak, Texas. He was born on 19 Mar 1875. He died on 18 Oct 1895 in Lone Oak, Hunt County, Texas. She married (2) WILLIAM C. DOWELL on 09 Aug 1898 in Lone Oak, Texas. He was born in Nov 1871 in Texas. He died in 1938 in Lone Oak, Hunt County, Texas.

  More About Alma R. Payne:
  Burial: 27 Feb 1941 in Lone Oak Cemetery, Hunt County, Texas
  Occupation: Bet. 1938-1940; Acting Postmaster of Lone Oak, Texas.

  Notes for Alma R. Payne:
  Funeral Service conducted by Dr. C. B. Jackson, Pastor of the First Baptist Church of Greenville.

 iii. NENA E. PAYNE was born in Jul 1885 in Lone Oak, Hunt County, Texas. She died in 1961 in Lone Oak, Hunt County, Texas. She married James V. Nash on 01 May 1904 in Lone Oak, Texas. He was born on 30 Jun 1877 in Texas. He died on 19 Jan 1938 in Lone Oak, Hunt County, Texas.

 iv. FLOYD ALEXANDER PAYNE was born on 15 May 1888 in Lone Oak, Hunt County, Texas. He died on 16 Sep 1966 in San Angelo, Texas. He married WILLIE WALSH.

She was born in 1892 in Texas.

31.   **ROBERT LEON**[6] **WEATHERLY** (Isaac C.[5], William W.[4], Isaac[3], William[2], Thomas[1]) was born on 20 Dec 1855 in Georgia. He died on 18 Apr 1943 in Hunt County, Texas. He married Mary Ann Hunt on 30 Sep 1879 in Lone Oak, Texas. She was born on 15 Feb 1861 in Hooker Ridge, Texas. She died on 17 Jul 1960 in Hunt County, Texas.

More About Robert Leon Weatherly:
Burial: Brigham Cemetery, Hunt County,
Texas
Occupation: Farmer

More About Mary Ann Hunt:
Burial: Brigham Cemetery, Hunt County, Texas

Robert Leon Weatherly and Mary Ann Hunt had the following children:

   i.   ROBERT CLAYTON[7] WEATHERLY was born on 29 Nov 1880 in Lone Oak, Hunt County, Texas. He died on 03 Jan 1952 in Hunt County, Texas. He married Ardella Myrtle Bonham on 20 Jun 1909 in Hunt County, Texas. She was born on 07 Jul 1883. She died on 18 Nov 1964 in Hunt County, Texas.

        More About Robert Clayton Weatherly:
        Burial: Caney Chapel Cemetery, Campbell, Texas

   ii.   ALBERT DAVID WEATHERLY was born on 05 Feb 1884 in Lone Oak, Hunt County, Texas. He died on 24 Jun 1940 in Hunt County, Texas. He married Carrie Ethyl Dodd on 07 Jun 1908 in Hunt County, Texas. She was born on 07 Sep 1887 in Lone Oak, Hunt County, Texas. She died on 06 Mar 1937 in Lone Oak, Hunt County, Texas.

        More About Albert David Weatherly:
        Burial: Hall Cemetery, Lone Oak,
        Texas
        Occupation: Barber
        Occupation: Farmer

   iii.   JOHN ISAAC WEATHERLY was born on 05 Aug 1886 in Lone Oak, Hunt County, Texas. He died on 05 Apr 1974 in Greenville, Texas. He married Rosa Edna Monroe on 01 Apr 1922 in Hunt County, Texas. She was born on 04 Aug 1900. She died in Jul 1980 in Greenville, Texas.

        More About John Isaac Weatherly:
        Burial: Memory Land, Greenville, Texas

   iv.   WILLIE BELL WEATHERLY was born in Jun 1889 in Lone Oak, Hunt County, Texas. She married IKE OVERSTREET.

   v.   LENA MAE WEATHERLY was born on 04 Apr 1893 in Hunt County, Texas. She died on 17 Dec 1969 in Hunt County, Texas. She married John Gath Ethridge, son of Samuel Ethridge and Rebecca Woodard on 09 Jun 1912 in Hunt County, Texas. He was born on 14 Aug 1885 in Clark County, Alabama. He died on 15 Aug 1962 in Hunt County, Texas.

More About Lena Mae Weatherly:
Burial: Brigham Cemetery, Hunt County, Texas

    vi.   HARRISON JOSEPH WEATHERLY was born on 09 Jun 1896 in Lone Oak, Hunt County, Texas. He married Emma Lou Harlow on 25 Aug 1920 in Hunt County, Texas.

32.   LILLIAN^6 WEATHERLY (Isaac C.^{5}, William W.^{4}, Isaac^3, William^2, Thomas^1) was born on 06 Oct 1858 in Cedertown, Georgia. She died on 09 Jul 1938 in Lone Oak, Hunt County, Texas. She married Thomas Jefferson Worthy on 19 Dec 1878 in Hunt County, Texas. He was born in 1846 in Georgia. He died on 27 Dec 1883 in Winnsboro, Texas.

More About Thomas Jefferson Worthy:
Occupation: County Clerk, Wood County, Texas
Occupation: Farmer
Military Service: Cavalry, C.S.A.

Thomas Jefferson Worthy and Lillian Weatherly had the following children:

    i.   ONIE^7 WORTHY was born in Oct 1880 in Winnsboro, Texas. She married David E. Mead on 29 Jan 1902 in Lone Oak, Texas.

    ii.   RACHEL MABEL WORTHY was born on 19 May 1884 in Winnsboro, Texas. She died on 15 Mar 1961 in Cleburne, Texas. She married James Lawrence Dean on 03 Jan 1906 in Lone Oak, Texas. He was born on 02 Jan 1883 in Garland, Texas. He died on 09 Jul 1957 in Cleburne, Texas.

        More About Rachel Mabel Worthy:
        Burial: Rosehill Cemetery, Cleburne, Texas

    iii.   TOMMIE WORTHY was born in Jun 1886 in Texas.

    iv.   ELLEN E. WORTHY was born in Texas.

33.   THOMAS MADISON^6 WEATHERLY (Isaac C.^{5}, William W.^{4}, Isaac^3, William^2, Thomas^1) was born on 28 Jan 1864 in Georgia. He died on 04 Apr 1935 in Lone Oak, Hunt County, Texas. He married Mae Elizabeth Cole, daughter of William Cole and Louisa Weeden on 03 Nov 1886 in Lone Oak, Texas. She was born on 11 Oct 1868 in Texas. She died on 15 Sep 1951 in Lone Oak, Hunt County, Texas.

More About Thomas Madison Weatherly:
Burial: Lone Oak Cemetery, Lone Oak, Hunt County, Texas
Occupation: Druggist
Occupation: Farmer

More About Mae Elizabeth Cole:
Burial: Lone Oak Cemetery, Lone Oak, Hunt County, Texas

Thomas Madison Weatherly and Mae Elizabeth Cole had the following children:

    i.   JESSIE MAUD^7 WEATHERLY was born on 19 Feb 1888 in Lone Oak, Hunt County, Texas. She died on 16 Aug 1964. She married Henry Wesley Stilwell, son of Thomas Stilwell and Mary Jones on 03 Nov 1909 in Lone Oak, Texas. He was born on 04 Aug 1886 in Lone Oak, Hunt County, Texas. He died on 29 Nov 1959 in Texarkana, Texas.

ii. JOSIE J. WEATHERLY was born on 02 Dec 1890 in Lone Oak, Hunt County, Texas. She died on 24 Sep 1958 in Lone Oak, Hunt County, Texas. She married O. Lee Fortenberry on 13 Apr 1913 in Hunt County, Texas. He was born on 16 Feb 1886. He died on 18 Jan 1962 in Lone Oak, Hunt County, Texas.

More About Josie J. Weatherly:
Burial: Lone Oak Cemetery, Hunt County, Texas

iii. HAZEL DELL WEATHERLY was born on 02 Nov 1897 in Lone Oak, Hunt County, Texas. She died on 12 Mar 1991 in Lone Oak, Hunt County, Texas. She married Audrey Beaird Trimble on 14 Apr 1918 in Hunt County, Texas. He was born on 17 Jun 1893. He died on 15 May 1949 in Lone Oak, Hunt County, Texas.

More About Hazel Dell Weatherly:
Burial: Lone Oak Cemetery, Hunt County, Texas

www.ingramcontent.com/pod-product-compliance
Lightning Source LLC
Chambersburg PA
CBHW080819280726
48660CB00018B/3534